RESEARCH METHODOLOGY IN PHYSICAL EDUCATION

RESEARCH METHODOLOGY IN PHYSICAL EDUCATION

Dr. A. MAHABOOBJAN

KALPAZ

Research Methodology in Physical Education

ISBN: 978-81-7835-874-1

Published in 2010 in India by
Kalpaz Publications
C-30, Satyawati Nagar,
Delhi-110052
E-mail: kalpaz@hotmail.com
Phone : 9212729499

Laser Type Setting by: Rudra Computer Graphics, Delhi
Printed at : Chawla Offset Printers, Delhi

Contents

Preface

This book has been written for the use as a basic test book of general and practical interest for those who venture to peep in to the realm of a most useful and fast growing subject Research. The students and people belonging to other fields and disciplines will also find the book informative as well as stimulating. Indeed it is a difficult task to present all the basic essential aspects of such a vast subject like research in to a limited number of chapters and pages of a brief text. However, an attempt is being made to present what is essential both from the angle of the scope of the subject as well as the needs and demands of the under-graduate and post-graduate courses of Indian Universities.

I express a deep sense of gratitude to my colleagues and my students who have been a source of constant inspiration to me. I also owe a debt of gratitude to my wife and daughter who assisted me in the preparation of the manuscript.

I hope that the book will prove to worthy and be of benefit to all those for whom it has been specifically designed. Any suggestions for its improvement will be gratefully acknowledged and appreciated.

Dr. A. Mahaboobjan

1

Meaning and Formations of Research

Meaning of Research

The term research has two parts "Re" and "Search". "Re" means again, "Search "means searching or seeking the fact or knowledge. So literally the term research means seeking the fact again and again. Etymologically it means seeking the solutions to the questions or to find answers to the question.

Scientifically speaking research is search for facts. The term research explore its meaning and its characteristics by the word "research" it self.

R - Stands for Rational way of thinking.

E - Stands for Expert and exhaustive treatment

S - Stands for Solutions

E - Stands for Exactness

A - Stands for Analytical analysis of data.

R - Stands for Relationship of facts.

C - Stands for Careful recording enquiry and Observation.

H - Stands for Honesty.

There are number of meaning attach to the word research it meaning may vary from person to person. Some important meanings are as follows.

1. Research is mainly concerned with exploration, experimentation and verification.
2. Research means a point of view, an attitude of enquiry.
3. Research is a systemic and scholarly application of scientific method.
4. Research means information in which we have confidence.
5. Research is a state of mind.
6. Research means a careful enquiry.
7. Research means a systemic and refined technique for obtaining a more adequate solution of a problem.
8. Research is an endeavor to discover, develop and verify the knowledge.
9. Research is a process of ascertaining principle.
10. Research is an honest and exhaustive intelligent searching for facts and principles.

Definition of Research:

According to Rusk," Research is a point of view an attitude of enquiry of a frame of mind. It ask questions which have better to not been asked, but it seeks to answer them by following a fairly definite procedure it is not a mere theorizing but rather an attempt to elicit facts and face to them one's they have been assemble".

Clifford wood defined research as "research is a careful enquiry examination in seeking facts or principles; a deligent, investigation to ascertain something".

J. Francis Rummel defines research as "Research is an endive to develop and verify knowledge. It is an intellectual process that has develops over hundred of years ever changing in purpose and form an always charging for truth.

Need and importance of Research in Physical Education:

Research is as old as academic consciousness of human mind. Research is an inseparable part of human knowledge. Its roll in human life is as precious as that of salt in a vegetable. The life would loose its taste without research exactly in the same manner as a vegetable without salt.

Research is an important prerequisite for progress. No progress without research. The shape of things and the order of the society shall continuously change. New innovations and invention shall be received with greater excitement and the process shall continue for ever. New knowledge, new inventions become known and eliminate the path of man's progress.

What is impossible in human life is become possible through research. What is unsearchable is searchable only through research.

The field of physical education and sports is mainly concerned with applied research and interdisciplinary research because physical education is suppose to study the body, mind, and sole in which one cannot be separated from other. In the same manner if you want to bridge the gap the interdisciplinary research with other areas like psychology, sociology, physiology, anatomy, bio-mechanics etc... are highly essential.

In this fast developing world fast approaching research is highly essential in physical education recreation and health education. Research is considered as more formal, systematic, intensive process of carrying on scientific method of analysis. Nowadays we are living in a fantastic world and individual can move for his break fast in one country and he can move for his lunch at another country. Similarly the scientific knowledge also come to immense of depth of knowledge of ocean.

Educational research is considered to be a prominent 'key' which is essential to be opinion new doors in physical education and sports. The following factors which are mainly concerned with need and important are as follows.

1. Research economize effort and increase efficiency:

Rusk describes this as "Research should accordingly by putting more scientific weapons at the disposal of the teacher, economize effort and increase efficiency. It is infact likely to head to what valued has termed leisurely method. The leisurely methods of today or fast as effective as the strenuous methods of the fact.

2. Research brings the confidence to the Teacher:

Rush write when the teacher technique is based on research teaching will no longer be regarded as one of the black horse, but will assume the status not as a decimal science but of progressive and elucidating procedure. The more highly stilled and better inform teacher will find new interest in his work and a new confidence in his own abilities.

3. Research leads to the adaptations of new methods:

Research will put and end to the criticism and rejection of old methods. If one is out prepare to assent the results of a method based on scientific research. One must repeat the investigation and disclose the new procedures and principles in fact area or field.

4. Research brings a sense of awareness:

The teacher who carries on an active research programme has at his command a sense of awareness and of deep understanding. He has at his finger tips eliminating examples and searching questions which can give his lectures or disclosure which may for real teaching.

5. To develop Research:

Research in physical education is a powerful fool and it begets research. It means research gives birth to another research. One research help and support to come out another research. Anumber of previous research study help and supported to go further research. Educational research brings vividness, completeness and comprehensiveness to complex problems in physical education and sports. It's makes our generalization more weighty, fruitful and effective.

6. To facilitate environmental conditions:

Today would awareness is to facilities environmental corny in their respective fields. In this area of research took a prominent role to develop the latest concept the whole would is full of in adequate and insufficiencies or prevailing. Wherever we go there we can find the latest awareness is to facilitate proper equipments and open new doors of research by introducing new environmental facilities.

7. To develop appropriate curriculum:

Curriculum designing is another problem the field of sports. Curriculum development should be taken place only through research, because curriculum should be defined on the basis of age, sex, past experience, and standard. To make the curriculum development more effective research should be conducted on the basis of scientific knowledge, the appropriate curriculum development can be desire.

8. To improve the methods of teaching:

Research is highly useful to improve the methods of teaching. Every research in this area brings new methods of teaching and coaching in physical education sports. Due to research new methods are introduced and the new methods may be developing totally and some time may be partially in their respective fields.

9. To develop better Thinking:

One of the letters of the term research is 'R' stands for a rational way of thinking. Thinking and imaginations are the two wings of a research to fly like birds. Thinking and imagination are prime sources of original research. So through this thinking philosophical research is also developed, because thinking is one of the aspects of philosophical research (i.e.) it is highly important to the physical educated persons to perceive these studies.

10. To explore new training schedule:

As it known research is a central factor for verification and explorations, to explore new training schedule and methods the field of physical education and sports, research is an inevitable too, without research no exploration and verification, (i.e.) research highly useful to the humanity to explore new areas.

11. To enhance professional's growth:

Research is made solution us for problems. To improve a protections and enrich it. Research is the basic concept in sports. It an area to be improved research should be improved first. It research is improved automatically it makes were generalization.

Scope of Research in Physical Education

The scope of research aims at discovering the truth. Research is under taken to discover answers to questions by applying scientific method. Aresearch maybe defines as a "careful critical enquiry or examinations in seeking facts or principles, deli gent investigation in order to assertion something".

With the discovery of new facts old conclusion or theories may either be rejected or modified. Research is necessary to examine the extent of the validity of the old conclusions or to findout some new facts and generalizations in connection with the exciting ones. Thus, it purpose (proclaim) to give a new direction and a new insides in to the exciting problem.

Neatly to say, a research must be based on some problem or some facts. Thus a constant search and research become essential to know the exact truth. The research may establish new empirical generalization and fulfill the old ones. Thus new theories are constructed.

The purpose of research is to unfold that truth by a systematic method. It may involve the manipulation of concept or simples in order to correct or verify the exciting knowledge or ideas, so that an operational generalization may be made the shape of a theory. A research may aim at the following things.

1. To find new generalization with old data.
2. To know old conclusions with new data.
3. To attempt to rich conclusions from the same set of data.
4. To find or to resolve contradiction exciting the area of study.

The following are the prime factors of the nature and scope of research in physical education and sports:

1. Identification of the Problem:

A research topic may variable selected from the burning problems of the time. It also be based on special interest and the confinement of the researcher. Atopic of research may take account the exciting information may gap in various theorious. Accordingly the researcher may choose his topic so that the information gape may be minimize.

2. Problem Solving:

Research is deligent and systematic enquiry and investigation to discover or reverse facts, theories and applications. Basically it is a matter of problem solving through application of the scientific method of enquiry. A problem in the research sense is not merely a reflex city or forestation of the kind encounter in daily living or in the course of one's work. Rather it is any protection question set forth for study and enquiry. Problem solving is a process in which, the rolls of the investigator are 1. Rezoning 2. Certainty and probability 3. Terminology 4. Basic assenting 5. The hypothesis etc. should be comprised.

3. Professional Contribution:

The problem should be worthy of time and effort needed to solve it in forms of making a distinct contribution to the professional field of interest. The scope must be brought of some significant to a segment of a profusion enough to provide specific answer to the question involve. Every fact of education is being challenge with respective relevance, thus research should be pertinent to correct and future procedure.

4. Testing the Hypothesis:

The third step in problem solving and the most important aspect in scope of physical education research is testing the Hypothesis aspect includes learning, making, and recording the observations (date), analyzing the data and drawing conclusion. This step uniquely characterizes the scientific method of problem solving. It reflex the rezoning of the practical mind. Hypothesis testing is a sensible strike forward process. The approach to testing a Hypothesis is determined by the nature of the problem the nature of methods of research etc.

5. Rendering service to society and humanity:

With record to educational research good and hat have pointed out that "Scientific work in education, psychology, and social sciences in general has and especially urgent obligation to play a social roll in rendering service, society and humanity.

6. Increase, Refinement and Development of the Quantum of knowledge:

It is the capital scope of educational research, investigator should be fully aware of the purposes to be served by the research which he undertakes. A dissertation has been made between fundamental or pure research and applied research. By pure or fundamental research is meant the investigation of problem in order to further and exciting knowledge.

7. Well Planned Education Research:

It is true that well planned education research will correctly be recording, limits are of course set by budget, government grand, management policies and educational priories, but it is always possible to find some ways of supporting well planned educational research process. A research define is a plane of the prepare research work. A research define is not a highly plane to be follow without deviation but rather a serious of guide post to keep one headed in the right direction.

8. Systematic research undertaking:

There are several problem area in education and physical education which headed to be explore by systematic research undertaking.

9. Research Eradicate the Educational Wastage:

Educational wastage, posses' serious challenge to the educator, wastage cannot be curved by lowering standard, of evaluation or by setting low pass makes. The causes of wastage and effective method of controlling by improved method of teaching and evaluation.

10. Roll of research to the social obligatory:

The school has a definable social obligation to the community which is Taught to Serve, how well this been done and what are to be done in order to better the social usefulness or schools need to be determined by research into various aspects of the problem for this resource it is definable that necessary for educational research should be asserted.

RESEARCH METHODS (OR) TYPES OF RESEARCH:

Educational research maybe classified under three categories, they are as follows:

1. Basic research (or) fundamental (or) pure (or) theoretical (or) library research.
2. Applied research (or) field research.
3. Action research (or) laboratory research.

Research has been classified differently depending upon the approach, the purpose and nature of research activity.

BASIC RESEARCH:

It is aimed at the discovery of basic truth or principle and is not immediately concerned with direct field application. The results of fundamental research are based as careful sampling procedures in order to extent the findings beyond the group or situation studies. This is a sophisticated kind of research which require a formal systematic process of carrying on the scientific methods of analysis and generalization. This kind of research can be conducted mainly by national educational organization or universities or some other higher educational institution. Fundamental research can take in shape in two different ways:

1. Discovery of a new thing.

2. Development of exciting theory.

Fundamental research entirely new theory the knowledge not existed so far. Such a discovery may follow from the researchers own idea or imagination.

In the excision theory by relaxing some of its assertions or by re-interpreting it or by developing a new theory with exciting one as it basis. Since the theory is based on assumption there often exists enormous scope of altering or formulation new dimensions to the exciting theory.

APPLIED RESEARCH:

Applied research is often called field research. It is concerned primarily, with establishing relationship and testing theory in the field setting, appling to other sample of the population from which the research subjects are taken.

Let as take an example of the medical institute to illustrate it. There the bio-chemistry lab may discover a medicine for a particular disease for result of fundamental research. The medical practitioner of the hospital may train out his medicine on several patients under different condition and find out the type of patient whom it affects positively and the condition under which it works well. Here the doctor is conducting a research which are may call applied research.

In schools the teacher faces several problem related to the instructional process. He leads to conduct research to solve the problem that affect the instructional process in his class or school. This is what we will call applied research.

ACTION RESEARCH:

Action research is the process by which practitioners attempt to study their problem scientifically in order to guide, correct and evaluate their decision and action is called action research. It is a systematic examination conducted by the group studying their own practices in research of sound answers to unsolved problem in their work and aim at improving their own performance at all their own jobs.

In the case of action research the person (Researcher (or) investigator) faces a problem and tries to find out it solution by searching is a scientific way through different lines of action. When a teacher focusses a problem in the class room he resorts to a number of process. Firstly he things about the nature of the problems and tries to visualize its proper properties. Then he things of the ways and means it solving it. Anumber of solutions come to his mind in the hypothetical form. He proceeds to take action on his hypothesis and tries to findout the action for the solution.

Action research is a continuous process which includes training out of a line of approach, recording the results. From this records this collected, he concludes that a particular approach more affective for developing comprehension. He makes it as his usual practice but his work on action research still continue new dimension to his problems and to his approach.

RESEARCH PROBLEM:

Research work is oriented towards the solution of a problem or to seek an answer by a question. The first step of a research process is to identify a problem. The selection of a problem in severed by reflective thinking and scientific thinking.

A research problem refers to some difficulty which a researcher experiences in the contact of either a theoretical or practical situation and wants to obtain a solution for the same.

A research problem on one which requires a researcher to find out the best solution for the given problem. I.e., to find out by which course of action the objective can be attained optimally in the context of a give in environment.

Criteria of Locating A Problem (or) Identification of A Problem

The identification and analyzing a research problem is the first and most crucial step of research process. A research problem can not be solved effectively unless a researcher possesses the intellect and insist to isolate and understand. The specific factors giving rise to the difficulty.

Since identifying the exact nature and dimensions of a problem is of major importance in research work, it is very essential that an investigator should learn how to recognize and define a problem. He should proceed step by step in locating the research problem.

1. Study of Literature:

(a) Text books (b) number of papers and disguises (c) Research quarterly.

2. Class room Discussions:

Discussions concerning a problem often produce information various ideas can be developed through such as exercise. In the class room they can interchange their ideas and discuss his problem with his colleagues and others who have enough experience in the same area or working on similar problems.

3. Systematically Record:

You should read all the problem and record one after one systematically on the basis of review, he should consider the priority field of the study.

4. Analyze Literature in an area or Subject field.

The available literature has been surveyed and examined with this area should be perceive my study or not.

5. Analyze thoroughly all the area of special interest:

Determining the field of research in which a researcher is keep interest to do the research work. The researcher should develop the mastery on the area or it should be in the field of his specialization.

6. Consider corroboration of former studies:

Verification and stresses the former studies. This would also help a researcher to know it there are certain gaps in the theories, or whether the existing theories applicable to the problem under study are in consistent it the theoretical expectations and so on. All these enable a researcher to take new stories in the field for furtherance of knowledge i.e. He can move up starting from the existing premise.

7. Examine controversial issues:

All the problem cannot be solved, so verify the controversial issues. Studies on related problems are useful for indicating the type of difficulties that may be encountered in the present study and also the possible analytical short comings. At times such studies may also suggest useful and even new lines of approach to the present problem.

8. Consult with faculty members:

People with rich experienced are in position to enlighten the researcher on different aspects of his proposed study and their advice and comments are usually invaluable to the researcher. They help his sharpen dis focus of attention on specific aspects with in the field.

9. Discover the interest of association and societies:

Pin point the interest in the specific aspect of the problem which is to be investigated.

CRITERIA FOR SELECTING THE PROBLEM:

The factors are to be considered the selection of a research problem both the criteria external and personal.

Before selecting the problem the following points to be kept inmind.

1. Is the problem interest to you:

Interest is the central factor otherwise nothing will happen with world. You should perceive the study, only if you interest in the problem.

2. It is possible to obtain appropriate data for the solution office problem:

It is possible to collect the data for the selected topic.

3. Are the techniques available for the selection of the problem?

The major purpose of techniques (or) special equipment is to define the process of observation on provide control of conditions and accuracy or permanence of recording.

4. Can the research be completed with the available time?

As a general rule a minimum amount of graduate work for the master degree is one year and for the doctor's degree three years.

The research completed within there limit.

5. The cost expenditure involved is feasible:

(a) Selection of subjects

(b) Purchasing of the equipments

(c) Convenience charges

(d) Remuneration for technical person.

(e) Photographer charges

(f) Miscellaneous expenses.

6. Do you have adequate training and experience to interpret result?

The researcher should have adequate training. The data under consideration must meet certain standard of accuracy, objectivity and verifiability.

7. With the problem make a significant contribution:

(i) does it add significantly to the field of knowledge

(ii) does it make a significant professionals contribution.

(iii) does it fit into exciting goes in correct knowledge.

(iv) does it open new avenues and closes of investigation.

(v) Is it likely to be met the standard required for publication.

CHARACTERISTICS OF GOOD RESEARCH

1. Research is directed towards the solution of a problem.
2. Research is based upon absorbable experience or empirical evidence.
3. Research is conducted only after all other sources of answers have been exhaustively examined.
4. Research demands accurate observation and description.
5. Research is directed to problems based on a "need to know"
6. Research involves gathering new data from primary of first hand sources or using existing data for a new purpose.
7. Research processes study presumed relations among natural phenomena. Studies are designed to either (1) establish relationship or (2) study observed relationship for the cause effect direction between or among variables.
8. Research requires expertise. The researcher knows what is already known about the problem and how others have investigated it.
9. Research strives to be objective and logical applying every possible test to validate the procedures employed, the data collected and the conclusions reached.
10. Research finding add to knowledge by providing new knowledge, communicating already existing knowledge is not to be considered as a research activity.

11. Research involves the quest for answers to unsolved problems.

12. Research is characterized by patient and unhurried activity.

13. Research is carefully recorded and reported.

14. Research is an orderly investigation that provides outcomes that withstand criticism of persons in the field.

15. Research can be thought of as a chain of reasoning, starting at problem formulation through investigation to findings.

DELIMITING AND LIMITING A PROBLEM

Delimitation:

It is the boundaries of the study. It reduces the problem to a workable size and set boundaries by limiting its scope. The restrictions on item like number of subjects and their age, number and kind of variables and other factors are shown in delimitations.

Limitation:

Factors which might affect the study and which are beyond the control of the research scholar are maintained under this heading. This includes cultural religions environmental and other factors which could not be controlled.

HYPOTHESIS

Hypothesis - Hypo + thesis

"Hypo" means tentative or subject to the verification. Thesis means statement about the solution of a problem.

One simply means a mess's assumption or some supposition to be proved (or) disproved.

Hypothesis is called a called a lamp into the dark. It is a brilliant guess about the solution of a problem.

Hypothesis is a inelegant guess hypothesis always thinking positively and it proves mostly passive way of approach by,

DIFINITION OF HYPOTHESIS:

"It is a tentative supposition or provisional guess which seems to explain the situation under observation"

James E Greisiton.

It is shrewd guess or inference that is formulated and provisionally adopted to explain observed facts or conditions and to guide in further investigation.

CHARACTERISTICS OF HYPOTHESIS:

1. Hypothesis shrewd be clear and precise. It the hypothesis is not clear and precise, the inference drawn on its basis cannot be taken as reliable.

2. Hypothesis shrewd be capable of being tested.

3. Hypothesis shrewd state relationship between variables, if it happens to be a relational hypothesis.

4. Hypothesis shrewd be limited in scope and must be specific.

5. Hypothesis shrewd be stated as for as possible in most simple terms, so that the same is easily understandable by all concerned.

6. Hypothesis shrewd be consistent with most known facts.

7. Hypothesis shrewd be amenable to testing with in a reasonable time.

8. Hypothesis must explain the facts that gave rise to the need for explanation. Thus hypothesis must actually explain what it claims to explain, it should have empirical reference.

TWO TYPE OF ERROR IN TESTING THE HYPOTHESIS

1. Type I error – hypothesis is rejected

2. Type II error – hypothesis is accepted.

1. It shown that obtained difference exists and not due change or sampling errors.

2. It indicates that obtained difference is due to change or sampling error.

FORMULATION OF RESEARCH HYPOTHESIS

Hypothesis is the basis of a scientific investigation education. It is the prolog the form any problem statement, it is generally possible to derive more than one hypothesis , there are three simple hypothesis generated from this problem to determine, the effect of massive, possible, verbal rewards on the reading achievement of children.

(a) Rewards increases reading achievement.

(b) Rewards decreases reading achievement.

(c) Rewards have no effect on the reading achievement.

Researcher formulate hypothesis using induction and deduction, one of the goals of researcher is to produce that pieces for generalized bodies of theory which will provide answers to practical problems. Hypothesis construction and testing enable researchers to generalize their findings beyond the specific condition which they were obtained.

Since a hypothesis is a formulation of anticipated findings, students are advised to develop a hypothesis as a means of demonstrating the basis for their study to themselves and their reader. The task of introducing a study and discussing the findings are facilitated by existence of a hypothesis.

Different Forms of Hypothesis (or) Different Types of Hypothesis

There are three forms (or) types of hypothesis

1. Declarative form
2. Null form
3. Question form

1. Declarative Form:

Generally states the relationship between the variables that the experimenter

Expects will emerge. (For example) The following hypothesis is stated in declarative form.

Eg. There will be a significant different on physical fitness among hockey players. The age group between 19 and 21 years as compare to football players.

2. Null form (or) Null Hypothesis:

A null hypothesis said no relationship exist between the variables consents.

Eg. There will be no Significant different among hockey players the age group between 19 and 21 as compare to football players.

3. Question Form:

We may state the hypothesis is a question form. Eg. The above said hypothesis is question form may read "In there any significant different on physical fitness among players as compare to football players.

LITERATURE SEARCH

The term literature refers to the knowledge of a particular area of investigation of any discipline which includes theoretical practical and its research studies.

NEED TO SURVEY OF RELATED LITERATURE

The phrase review of literature consists of two words Review and Literature.

The term review means organize the knowledge of the specific area of research to evolve an edifice of knowledge to show that his study would be an addition to this field.

A researcher must read related literature to avoid a problem that has already been investigated. At the same time a researcher can adopt a technique that is employed in a former researcher work. A critical study an earlier work may be helpful to a researcher to do his research work perfectly.

The task of review of literature is highly creative and tedious because researcher has to synthesize the available knowledge of the field in a unique to provide the rationale for his study.

The review of literature provides some in light regarding strong points limitations of the preview studies.

Definition

The literature in any field forms the foundation upon which all future work will be built. If we fail to build the foundation of knowledge provided by the review of literature our work is likely to be shallow and will often duplicate work that has already been done better by some one else.

W.R. Brog.

"Practically all human knowledge can be found in books and libraries. Unlike other animals that must start a new write each generation, man builds upon the accumulated and recorded knowledge of the past. His constant adding to the vast store of knowledge as ekes possible progress in all areas of human endeavours.

John W. Best.

Need and role of Related Literature

The search of related literature should be completed before the actual conduct of the study begins. This stage serves several important functions.

1. A knowledge of related research enables investigators to define the frontiers of their field.

2. A review of related theory and research enables researchers to place their questions in perspective.

3. One should review the literature for the purpose of finding a link between one's study and the accumulated knowledge is one's field of interest.

4. Hovering selected literature helps researchers to revise their question and to classify and fine the concepts of the study that it can be investigated.

5. A critical review of related literature often heads to insist in to the reasons for contradictory result in an area.

6. Through studying related research, investigators learn which methodologies have proved useful and which learn less promising.

7. A through research through related researches avoids unintentional replications of previous studies.

8. The study of related literature places researchers in a better position to interest the significance of their own result.

Objectives of Review of Literature

The review of literature serves the following purposes.

1. It provides theories, ideas, explanations or hypothesis which may prove useful in the formulation of a new problem.

2. It indicates whether the evidence already available solves the problem adequately without requiring further investigation. It a voids the replication.

3. It provides the sources for hypothesis. The researcher can formulation research hypothesis on the basis of available studies.

4. It suggests method, procedure, sources of data and statistical techniques appropriate to the solution of the problem.

5. It locates comparative data and findings useful in the interpretation and discussion of results. The conclusions drawn in the related studies may be significantly compared and may be used as the subject for the findings of the study.

6. It helps in developing experts and general scholarship of the investigator in the area investigated.

7. It contribution towards the accurate knowledge of the evidence or literature in one's area activity is a good avenue towards making one self.

MAJOR LITERATURE SOURCES

There are various sources which have to be located and studied.

The sources can be classified in to,

1. Primary Sources or Critical Literature:

First hand source of data in research, the original study. This means the studies which has got direct relationship and are apt for this study. This helps to formulate the hypothesis and developing a creditable theoretical frame work of the study.

2. Secondary Sources or Applied Literature:

Sources of data in research in which an author has evaluated and summarized previous research. This involves those studies that are related to the investigation but are more peripheral than central in nature (indirect relationship). This is important because they provide the background upon which it rests.

It can also be classified in to direct and indirect sources.

Direct Sources:

In the field of physical education, the direct sources of formation are educational journals, books, monographs, bulletins, yearbooks, dissertations and thesis and government publications.

Indirect Sources:

The indirect sources are available in the form of directories and bibliographies, abstracts, indexes, encyclopedias, miscellaneous, sources, question sources, bibliographical references etc.

LIBRARY SOURCES:

Some of the library sources that are used for the search are books, journals and periodicals.

Abstracts

Encyclopedias

Specializes Dictionary

Dissertation and Thesis

Bibliographies

Micro fiche (micro form publications)

Card catalog

Hand books and Year books

News Paper, Conference, Seminar Papers.

Computer / Internet Sources.

2

Historical Research

TYPES OF RESEARCH METHODS:

Research methods can be categorized in to three basic types. The meanings and their further classification have been given as follows:

1. HISTORICAL METHOD:

It describes "What was". This is concerned with the past and which attempts to trace the past events as a means of seeing the present in perspective.

This method can be classified in to three types.

(a) Historical (b) Legal (c) Documentary

2. SURVEY METHOD:

It describes "What is". This is concerned with the present and attempts to determine the relationships between existing non-manipulated values.

This method can be classified into four types.

(a) Descriptive (b) Analytical (c) School surveys (d) Genetic survey.

Descriptive survey further classified in to three types.

(a) Survey testing method (b) Questionnaire method (c) Interview method

Analytical survey further classified in to five types

(a) Documentary frequency (b) Observational (c) Rating (d) Critical incident (e) Factor analysis.

3. EXPERIMENTAL METHOD:

It describes "What will be". It focus is towards the discovery of basic Relationship among phenomena as means of predicting and controlling their occurrence.

This method can be classified in to four types,

(a) Simple experimental designs (b) Mulatto – Variate analysis (c) Case study and (d) Predictive or correlation.

SURVEY RESEARCH :

Survey method is a systematic collection of analysis interpretation and recommendation of facts concerning some aspects of current situation. E.g. Institution, Sports, Students, Census. The survey must be purposeful properly defined and delimited, planned expertly conducted any systematically presented or interpreted concerned with describing a specific set of phenomena at one phenomena at one point in time.

Survey does not aspire to develop an organised body of scientific laws but provide information useful to the solution of local as well as universal problems. The collected data must be relevant, objective, reliable, and representative of the population. No profession, not even physical education and sports, can hope to prosper unless there is periodic introspection of the strength and weaknesses of its policies and evaluation of the programmes regularly. Hence survey is an essential ingredient of the total process of research in physical education and sports.

SURVEY BY QUESTIONNAIRE AND INTERVIEW :

The purpose of broad survey is to obtain responses from a large number of individuals who could not be interviewed personality within a short period of time without considerable expense. The instrument for the broad survey is questionnaire. E.G Topics may be national, regional or state level.

The Questionnaire

Questionnaire is not of the most extensively used data gathering techniques with the researches concerned with descriptive type of problems. "A questionnaire is a questions of logically arranged in sequence and used when factual information is needed",- Best.

Can gather information of status (of individual and groups) and expert opinion (of deans, head of the departments and coaches) and authoritative opinion (individual with outstanding qualifications).

Questionnaire is a systematic compilation of questions that are submitted to a sampling of population from which information is desired. In survey questionnaire is the best tool of data collection because the classified information needed can be collected only through a set of battery of questions.

Development of a Questionnaire

1. The researcher must have training experience and he must know the purpose and objective of his study.

2. The questionnaire must serve the purpose for which it is constructed.

3. It should obtain factual data, rather than opinion.

4. The questions should be arranged in a logical order.

5. A trial run of the questionnaire may be made on friends to see whether it works.

6. Every question should be precise, relevant, clear and easy to understand.

7. The question should be as brief as possible.

8. When questions are called for opinions, some form of the Likert scale is helpful –(Strongly disapprove disapprove – undecided – approve – strongly approve).

9. Specific terms which could be misinterpreted easily, must be defined and explained. For e.g. intramural, athletics, football etc.

10. As far as possible descriptive adjectives and adverbs should be avoided.

11. Double negative should be avoided.

12. The researcher must consult professors and experts while classifying areas of information and framing questions.

13. Aviod sensitive questions E.g. married –divorced.

14. Biased questions should not be asked. For e.g. "athletics are always harmful to children".

15. Better not to be ask incomplete questions. For e.g. Isometric exercise contribute most"- to what or compared with what.

16. Should not construct lengthy questions and too difficult questions. e.g. calculate the percentage of students who participate in intramurals.

Trial Run:

The purpose of trial run is to discover if the meaning of all statements on the questionnaire are clear and adequate to obtain the desired information. Get the advise from staff and friends.

Tabulation:

Modify and rearrange the questionnaire if needed.

Rewriting:

Again revise the questionnaire based upon the information obtained from the elders.

Appearance of Questionnaire or Characteristics of Questionnaire

(a) The paper can be any attractive colours and of 81/2" x 11".

(b) The major headings should be larger than the sub-headings. Printed forms are better than typed forms. Avoid cheap paper and ditto questions.

(c) Provide adequate space for answers and it should be clear, complete concise and explicit. For an objective response parenthesis.

(i) ( ) or may be used.

(d) First page name and address of the investigator, complete instruction for filling and returning and the purpose the must be given clearly. A place for the name and address of the person replying must be provided.

(e) The questionnaire should not be very long or very short. Arrange in a logical order.

Administration of Questionnaire

The primary difficulty is to obtain an adequate response. So the researcher should follow some procedures to encourage the greatest possible return.

1. Enclose in the mailing a stamped self-addressed envelope and a covering letter stating the purpose (partial fulfillment of the masters degree)

2. Ask for willingness to know the results.

3. Must avoid asking questions of sensitive in nature (salary rating of teachers etc.) and should write that the replies will be kept confidential.

4. Should be sent in an appropriate time.

5. Before sending the questionnaire, send an advanced letter and self addressed card and ask for willingness.

6. The most valuable device that may be used to obtain maximum number of responses is the follow-up. Five follow-ups at the intervals of 2 weeks after mailing the questionnaire is followed.

   (i) First follow up: Send a post card after 2 weeks.

   (ii) Second follow up: At the end of the 4th week, send a copy of the original covering letter and a copy of the questionnaire for those who has not replied to the first mailing.

   (iii) Third follow up: At the end of the 6th week, a separate letter is sent to those who have not replied so far.

   (iv) Fourth follow up: At the end of the 8th week send a personalized letter indicating the desire to receive the response. Again send a self addressed envelope also to facilities immediate response.

   (v) Fifth follow up: Send a personalized letter with or without another questionnaire after another two weeks. This would be the final appeal and should result in the maximum number of returns.

INTERVIEW

This is a better method of obtaining survey information than the questionnaire. Here the researcher gathers data directly from individuals in face contact. This is a formal between two individuals- the interviewee who is the giver and the interviewer who is the seeker. The interviewee is not supposed to give a written reply to the investigator's questions. This is a direct way of collecting certain types of data- both quantitative and qualitative.

Interview needs careful planning. First, he must determine as to what information he needs further. Second, questions must be constructed as clearly as possible and arranged in a logical sequence. Third, to have written schedule of questions is virtually rewarding. Memory may betray third interview. Fourth, questions may be asked in their natural form but indirect or biased form. Lastly it should be prepared carefully.

Uses of the interview:

1. The interview helps to get confident information (When you send a questionnaire they may not give the confidential information). He should assure them that the information will be kept confidential.

2. Able to draw out the information by on-the-spot-follow-up questions which is not possible through questionnaire method. For e.g. practices in athletics and operation of budget.

3. The interview permits the interpretation of the meaning of questions. But in questionnaire the question may still be misunderstood or certain concepts misinterpreted.

4. The investigator can form some judgement of the adequacy of replies (can avoid dishonesty) e.g. Do you have intramural programme?

5. The interview survey affords an opportunity for the interview to give information and to develop rapport with the respondent. If this is done properly the response will be much better.

6. This s appropriate when dealing with young children, illiterate, those with language difficulties and those with limited intelligence.

7. Sports psychologists and sports sociologists use interview for gathering data. Such as psycho-dynamics, motives, needs, drives, competitive spirit, aptitudes, aptitudes, adjustment, problems, athlete – coach relationship etc.

Disadvantage of Interview

1. It is time Consuming
2. It is a costly affair especially when respondents are scattered.
3. Higher officials do not grant interviews.
4. Defeated athletes hate interviews
5. Inexperienced and biased interviewer makes interview dull, hopeless, boring and monotonous.

HISTORICAL RESEARCH:

Historical research is proceeds supplementary to observation in which the researcher seeks to test the authenticity of the reports or observation made by other.

This is the systematic collection and objective revaluation of data related to past occurrences to determine causes, effects or trends of there events that may help explain present events and anticipates future events.

HISTORICAL STUDY

History gives information of part events. There is no story teller. Who fills in historic gaps from his imagination. Historical studies are similar to experimental studies for it gives information with accuracy and validity.

AIMS OF HISTORICAL RESEARCH

- History relates to the heritage of any field.
- It established professional depth tradition and customs
- It relates to the growth and development of the field.
- It relates to the problem faced and solve.
- It relates to the cultural for ever exerted.
- It relates to the movement that have wanted and persisted.
- It reflects to changes in implements facilities and customs.
- It beings into highlight thoughts and deeds of the pioneered and leaders who shaped the profession, nation etc.

In earlier days historians wrote history merely to glorify an event and used it as a tool for propagating the event. History as a science was generally unknown in the 19th century.

As the years rolled by historical studies became basically scientific they are.

- Critically and objectively searched the primary and secondary sources.
- Historical formulated and evaluated the hypothesis.
- Tentative explanations of the occurrence of the events are made.
- Unlike experimental studies the historical hypothesis cannot be tested.

- Historians cannot employ control observation.
- In historical studies the original events cannot be repeated (or) reentered.
- Historical science reconstructs the human science and judges its meaning so as to get the true facts.
- Historical evidence can be evaluated.
- Historical method realizes the cause and effect relationship.

STEP INVOLVED IN HISTORICAL RESEARCH:

1. Selection of the problem
2. Formulation of hypothesis or questions.
3. Collection of vita data through primary and secondary sources. Evaluate source materials.
4. Analysis of data through internal and external criticism.
5. Preparation of report in reliable form and interpret findings.

SOURCES OF HISTORICAL DATA

Data is information organized for analysis or used as a basis for a decision. The researcher should collect adequate and accurate information of the past. Historical data are classified as follows.

1. PRIMARY SOURCES:

"A primary source gives the words of the witnessed or the first recorder of an event. It includes manuscript, archives, letters, diaries and speeches.

Primary sources which are,

EYE or EAR witness accounts original objects.

It is first hand information such as the testimony of an eye witness, an original document or description of a study written by the person who conducted it would be considered in primary source.

It may be a living individual who was a real participant in the event.

Eg: a soldier, a leader, an athlete or a sportsman

They are the original information or materials.

The Most Common Primary Sources Are,

1. **Official Records:**

   State, district and national associations have minutes of meetings, reports of committees, annual reports, official documents, budgets, honors, awards made, and attendance records, paper presented, state syllabus, published materials, laws, court proceedings and decisions.

2. **Personal Records:**

   They are letters, diaries, autobiographies, lecture notes, diplomas and honorary degrees.

3. **Oral Statements:**

   The family stories told and other eye witness superstitutians, rituals, accounts of events as told by the beholder are called as oral statement.

4. Published Materials:

Syllabus and courses of study, other such sources, newspaper accounts, pamphlets, year books, awards, magazine stories and formal stories.

5. Pictorial Records:

These are photographs, movies, drawings paintings and sentpture.

6. Physical Records:

Buildings, facilities, apparatus and equipments.

7. Printed Materials:

Text books, report cards, newspaper advertisements and certificates.

8. Mechanical Records:

Tape recordings of interviews, meetings and speeches and video recordings.

SECONDARY SOURCES:

Secondary sources are the descriptions of primary sources and are supporting sources. They are not first hand reports, they are written by persons who did not live in the period under study or who were not indirect contact with the events.

Secondary sources which are,
Copies of objects
Second hand information

It is second hand information such as the description of historical events by some one not present, when the event occurred it would be considered secondary source. More than one mind comes in between the original happening. Eg: Book about him.

The most common secondary sources of historical data are,

1. Text books 2. Encyclopedia 3. News papers 4. Periodicals 5. Reviews of research and other referenced.

HISTORICAL CRITICISM:

This process by which the historical researcher weeks out the unwanted materials from the collected evidence, is known as historical criticism. The researcher weighs, considers, criticizes, examines the evidences before be accept, and rejects.

The primary and secondary historical sources should be critically analysed and examined because :

1. A remain may not be genuine
2. A record may not be correct
3. A Photograph may be faked and
4. A Speech may have been written by a ghost writer.

Historical research requires a systematic data evaluation of the evidence. The historical materials must be evaluated by applying two types of criticism. They are :

1. External criticism 2. Internal criticism.

EXTERNAL CRITICISM:

It establishes the genuineness and authority of data. It determines whether a given source is genuine and admissible as evidence.

For this a number of qualities will serve to clarity this form of:

1. Does the language and writing style consist to the period in question and is it typical of other work done by the author?
2. Is there evidence that the author exhibits ignorance of things or events that she/he should have known?
3. Did the author report things, event or place that could not have been known during that period.
4. Has the original manuscript been altered either unintentionally or internationally by copying?
5. Is the document an original or draft copy?
6. If the manuscript in un dated or the author, unknown, is there any clues internally as to its origin?

   Eg. Physical education remains eg. Bats and hats.

   (Whether it is artificial product (or) made by human being)

INTERNAL CRITISM:

It determines if the contents of a document are accurate. This is concerned with the meaning and accuracy of statements. For their number of question will serve to clarify this form of criticism.

1. What was meant by the author by each word and statement?
2. How much credibility can the author be given?

3. What was the author trying to say?

4. How could the author's words be interpreted?

3

Philosophical Research

PHILOSOPHICAL STUDY

Philosophical study is a school of wisdom it is a criticism of knowledge. According to John Deway-Philosophical is a generalized through of criticism. Its ultimate value of life experience is that it continuously provides instinct for the criticism of value (or) belief instructions action that are formal in all aspects of experiences.

According to john. W. best Philosophy is a study of processes that govern thought and conduct of the principles (or) laws that regulate the universe under the reality.

Philosophy studies are used for resolving the problem (i.e.) problems that cannot be currently solved by other things (or) that cannot wait on other means for an answer.

The Philosophy method can be applied to problem at once without approaching the experiment it takes time, but it is prone to be wrong, through Philosophical study the objective of education the organization of education the organization of curriculum content of course selection of methodology are established norms than through scientific mean for we are aware that the educational system is planned for democratic purpose hence the ideology of the society is set by Philosophical basis even before the object are set.

Philosophical studies are required for physical education health education and recreation to establish vision of ultimate ends.

Eg: the value of two types of exercises for the development of strength to be composed the appropriate method to be applied will be experimental study. But if the status of HPERD is to be determined by applying the tools of survey methods. The status is to resolved hence Philosophical methods can be applied to a problem at once without the experimental so Philosophical solution is timely (prone) to be wrong than solutions by the experimental study.

Philosophical studies are needs in education, which of course include the aims and objectives of physical education, Philosophical sports curriculum content selection of teaching, methodology are often critical examined subjected for Philosophical includes.

- Aesthetics: a science which deals with beauty of life arts and doctrine of facts.
- Ethic: science of moral (or) rules and contact to note right and wrong.
- Logic: science of reasoning.
- Metaphysics: science deals with principle of law which governs the universe.

In the critical thinking there are maximal pole and minimal pole content of thinking continuous maximal pole contend of thinking required maximum amount of critical thinking and minimum amount of scientific evidence, available to guide that thinking upon which base results got from memory from theory of nervous muter reaction.

Aims and Objectives Philosophical Research

The philosophical research is conducted to establish truth or reality. Education has two aspects theoretical and practical. The practical enriched by scientific researches and theoretical aspect can be developed by conducting philosophical researches.

Philosophical method is used for resolving problems, especially problems that currently cannot be solved by other means.

NATURE OF PHILOSOPHICAL RESEARCH

1. The philosophical method is largely subjective since the solution of the problem is accomplished through critical thinking based on evidence.

2. Philosophical is the study of processes than govern thought and conduct principles and leave that regulate the universe.

3. It takes its essence from aesthetics, logic, ethics and metaphysics.

4. Philosophical research involves critical thinking and makes the treats of possible use of experience.

5. Philosophy should guide in arriving at reasonable and consistent solution to problem in every day practice.

STEPS IN PHILOSOPHICAL RESEARCH

1. Defining and delimiting the problem.
2. Collecting available facts related to the problem.
3. Analyzing the facts to identify relationships among them.
4. Deriving general principles that describe the relationships hidden in the principles.
5. Stating these principles in the form of hypothesis.
6. Critically test hypothesis for acceptance, rejection or modification.

THE CRITICAL THINKING CONTINUEM

The philosophical research rests heavily on the application of critical reasoning. In philosophical studies knowledge is assembled and critical thinking is applied, some studies may need high degree of thinking. So the degree of reliance upon critical thinking applied to studies may be considered on a continuem with a maximal and minimal pole.

MINIMAL POLE

The minimal pole of the critical thinking continuum is the pole with the minimal amount of critical amount of critical thinking upon which to base results. During experimentation, science will be dominant. However, critical thinking will be evidence when interpretations are made and conclusions are drawn.

MAXIMAL POLE

The maximal pole of the critical required the maximal amount of critical thinking and the minimal amount of scientific evidence available to guide that thinking.

PHILOSOPHICAL METHOD

Philosophical method is based on critical thinking criticism does not end with mere intellectual discrimination it forms experience from both empirical and scientific observation.

- Philosophy determines aims and objective of physical education and sports.
- Philosophy criticizes beliefs and values.
- Physical education attempts to idealize individuals and institutions.
- It helps all scientific enquiry.
- Physical education is contemplative.
- Physical methods by it self not science.
- It is analytical in nature.
- Physical method is used to resolve certain problem.
- Physical method is largely subjective for the solution of problem is obtained through critical thinking.
- Physical method is based on logical procedure that controls the processes of experimentation and statistical analysis.
- It governs thought and content of the principle and laws that regulate universe.
- It underlines all knowledge and reality.
- Physical method may be credibility and reliability when compared and to experimented.

- Physical education method is systematic discipline of value and of underlying assumption.
- Philosophical method user the expert results as evidences for resolving the problem.
- Philosophical involves ascertain consideration of alternative choice with in the frame work of the content.

ACCORDING TO JOHN DEWEY

Philosophical method indicates a close association between philosophy and science. No scientific work can be undertaken without critical thinking. Philosophy basically gathers existing evidence for reapproaching the hypothesis where as the scientific study cases the experimental procedure. There are Five steps John Dewey was tested for philosophical study.

- The occurrence of felt difficulty.
- Delimitation of different terms used in studying the problem.
- Necessary explanation for hypothesis.
- Collection of data.
- Analysis and testing the hypothesis.

STEPS INVOLVED IN PHILOSOPHICAL METHOD

- Identify the problem area, the problem is defined and delimited.
- Collect available facts related to the problem.
- Analysis the facts and working them into pattern and directly relationship among them.

- From these patterns derives general principles that describes.
- The relationship inherent in the principle.
- State those principles in the form of hypothesis.
- Test the hypothesis for acceptance, rejection and modification.

CASE STUDIES

The case study is a complete analysis and report of the particular individual, family, subject, school, institution, club, play ground, or community with a view to ensure the possible improvement.

It attempts to examine an individual or unit in depth.

On the other hand the aim of case study is to understand the life cycle of an individual an institution or a social group or community.

The case study is a diagnostic study. Many case studies arise from endeavours to solve problems. The greatest advantage of case study is the possibility of dept; it attempts to understand the whole community or the whole adult in the totality of that individuals environment.

The case study is individuals, may be done on great scientists, artists, under standing sports persons etc.

What is Case Study?

The case study is potentially the most valuable method known for obtaining a true and comprehensive picture of an individual.

Characteristics of a good Case Study:

1. It should be based on adequate and complete data.

2. Its date should be valid.

3. It should have continuity about it.

4. It record should be kept confidential.

5. It date should be scientifically synthesized and this synthesis should be as much prognostic as diagnostic.

6. It follow up worth should be under taken.

STEPS IN THE CASE STUDY TECHNIQUE

The researcher should adopt the following steps when undertaking research using the case study.

1. Selection of Case

The initial step in a case study is to define the nature of the strength or weakness to be studied and to select the case or cases most exemplary of the factors studied.

2. Determining Status of the Phenomenon

The status of the phenomenon under investigation must be determined either by direct observation or measurement.

3. Hypothesis

After determining the status of the phenomenon the researcher should formulate a tentative hypothesis which will guide him for data collection on the individual cases.

4. Data Collection

Data collected by the researcher should be such that are relevant to his problems.

Data may be gathered by a wide variety of method, including the follows.

(i) Observations

Is one of the most important techniques of collecting data in case study. This may be personally done by the researcher. With this one can get the information about the physical characteristics, social qualities like co-operation adjustment, sociability and behavior. Information can be got from friends, teachers, relatives, coach and team members. The observations should be recorded orally or in writing.

(ii) Interview

The researcher interviews the subject, his relatives friends, class-mates, coaches, teacher etc. so as to gather comparable information.

(iii) Materials

Documents, records, digress, diplomas, and wards could be collected. So as to get information about the physical status health conditions, educational status. E.g. medals and prizes received at various levels.

(iv) Photographs

Photographs, videos, movies and audio recordings would act as a tool.

(v) Psychological tests and inventories:

The collection of data with the above depends on the type of study conducted. The 'case' himself can fill in the questionnaire or other individual may be asked to give their opinion through opinionnaies. Better to combine both the technique to get truthful data. Questionnaire such as cattles 16 P.F., MPI, EPI and MMPI are used successfully to collect unique and ordinary informations.

(vi) Achievements Record:

Newspaper, school records and school magazines would give many details. Newspaper carry reports on the play patterns, techniques, achievements and performance outstanding athletes and players.

Disadvantages of Case Study

1. Getting appointments with the 'unique' people is too difficult.
2. The independent variables cannot be manipulated.
3. Subjects cannot be randomly assigned to treatment groups.

Advantages of Case Study

1. Replication is possible as in experimental research. Replication is a "synthesis of repetition and duplication". The main aim is challenging and verifying the conclusions of some previous study.
2. The questionnaires used are valid ones.

NATURE OF CASE STUDY DATA:

The data may be collected under the following heads.

Psycho Physical Examination:

Vision, hearing, speech, neuromuscular co-ordination.

Medical Examination:

Height, weight ratio, nutrition, teeth, general health bodily disease alignment, disease or disturbance of the nervous and glandular system, worms, adenoids.

Mental Conditions:

General intelligence through verbal, non-verbal tests, special abilities.

Temperamental Aspects:

General anatomical complexes, neurosis, interests, attitudes or sentiments, character.

Health History:

Conditions of pregnancy and birth dates of talking\, walking dentition, school, puberty, accidents, illness, operations, family life.

Educational Testing:

Reading, number hand writing, composition, capacity for sustained application attitude special skill or knowledge general information and culture.

School History:

Promotion, kind of work done mobility, analogy of schools attended relations with teachers.

Family History:

Ancestry, Parents, siblings, home conditions, economic status and History, culture resources, relations with in home, control attitude of parents towards the society.

Social History:

Contacts attitude towards own religion mixing with children of the same age undesirable company, sex, history, delinquency etc.

4

Experimental Research

RESEARCH DESIGN

Experimental design refer to the conceptual frame work with in which the experiment in conducted.

An experimental design serves two functions: (1) It establishes the condition for the comparison required by the hypothesis of the experiment and (2) It enables the experimenter through statistical analysis of the data to make a meaningful interpretation of the results of the study.

"Experimental research in defined as observation under controlled conditions"

Experimental method is a scents for method. It proved a systematic and logical method for answering and question.

DIFFERENT RESEARCH DESIGN

Research design may split in to the following parts.

1. Sampling Design:

It deals with the methods of selecting items to be observed for the given study.

2. Observational Design:

Relates to the conditions under which the observations are to be made.

3. Statistical Design:

It concerns with the question of how many items are to be observed and how the information and data gathered are to be analyzed.

4. Operational Design:

It deals with the techniques by which the procedures specified in the sampling, statistical and observational design can be carried out.

VARIABLES

"Variables are the contributions or characteristics that experimenter manipulates, controls or observes".

There are five types of variables. They are

1. Independent variables
2. Dependent variables
3. Categorical variables
4. Control variables
5. Extraneous variables

1. It is otherwise called experiment of the treatment variables. It is part of experiment that the researcher in manipulating. It is otherwise called cause set up by the researcher.

2. It is also called as criterion variable. The dependent variable is what is measured to assess the effects of the independent variables.

3. It is called as moderator variable. It is a kind of independent variable that cannot be manipulated because it is categorized by age, sex and soon.

4. It is a factor that control possibly influence the result and that is kept and if the study.

5. It is a factor that control effect the relationship between the independent and dependent variables. But that cannot included or controlled.

EXAMPLE:

Effect of send running on endurance performance of college man. In the above example all the variable can be identified.

Independent variables	-	Sand running
Dependent variables	-	Endurance
Categorical variables	-	college man
Control variables	-	In the above study fitness level of the subjects can be controlled by a pre physical working capacity test. So in this manner the difference in fitness can be controlled.

Extraneous variables - the external factor such as climate, diet and various background of the subjects are not controlled. This might influence the result of the study.

EXPERIMENTAL DESIGN

Experimental design in the blue print of the procedures that enables the researcher to carryout the research. There are various types of experimental designs. The selection of a particular design depends upon such factors as the nature and purpose of the experiment. Type of the variables to be manipulated and the nature of the date, the facilities or the condition for carrying out the experimental and capabilities of the investigator.

TYPES OF EXPERIMENTAL DESIGN

There are many types of experimental designs. They are

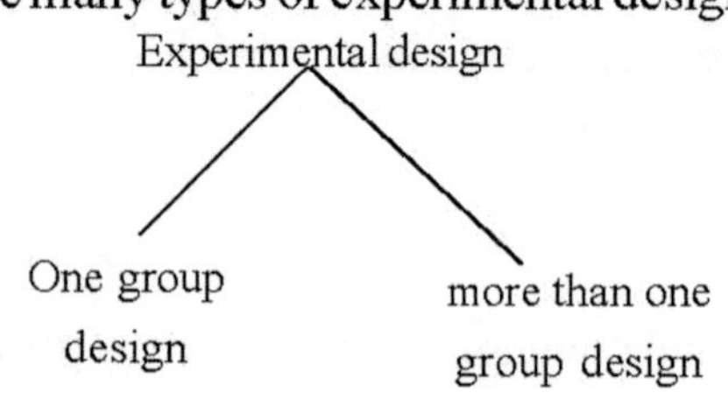

One group design	More than one group design
1. Single group design	1. Static group comparison design
2. Reverse group design	2. Random group design
3. Repeated group design (Rotational group design)	3. Related group design

1. ONE GROUP DESIGN

This is otherwise called as simple group experimental designs because they are relatively uncomplicated. They lead to problem solution in a direct manner. It is easy to administrate and this involve less complicated techniques of data gathering.

(i) Single group design

This involves only one group of subjects. The experimental variable will be applied (conditioning). If the initial Mean (M_1) is improved to the final Mean (M_2) after six weeks period of conditioning, and the differences (M_2 -M_1) is statistically significant, the investigator will be able to prove that this difference in the mean was due to the physical conditioning given by the investigator.

Eg: Effect of conditioning on middle distance running.

Procedure: A group of subjects were conditioned for six weeks in middle distance running. Different tests were conducted on muscular strength, endurance and speed at the beginning before the conditioning was given and the results were noted. This is the initial performance (M). After the training period again the same tests were conducted and the results were noted. This is the final performance (M_2). The differences of (M_2 - M_1) showed significant difference. Hence it is proved that the conditioning had improved the muscular strength, endurance and speed by decreasing the time in running.

Statistical Procedure

t-test is applied because only two means are involved.

Advantage

1. This design does not require the equation or rotation of groups.

2. This is particularly well adapted to classroom situation.

3. Only one group is needed.

Disadvantages

1. There is no control group to compare and establish the effectiveness of the application of experimental variables.
2. Full effect cannot be ascertained.
3. Not suitable for maturation and growth studies (adolescent period).

(ii) Reverse group design.

This design is a variation of the single group. Here also only one group is used. After the initial test, an experimental variable (A) is applied for a period of six weeks. Then the subjects are retested. Now another variable (B) is applied for a period of six weeks to the same group. Then the subjects will be tested again (final) and the improved will be noted. This will give the combined effect of both the variables. Initial test-factor A- Re-test- Factor B-Final test.

Eg: Effect of rhythmics and asanas on flexibility.

Procedure: A group of subjects will be selected and tested for flexibility (goniometer) (Initial test) (M_1). Then the experimental factor A-rhythmics will be given for a period of six weeks. Immediately now the other factor B- asanas will be given for the same group for a period of another six weeks. Now the final test will be taken (M_2). The difference between the final test and the initial test will give the combined effect of rhythmics and asanas on flexibility (M_2 - M_1).

Statistical Procedure: t-test is used because only two means are to be compared.

Advantages:

1. Fewer subjects are needed.

2. Combined effect of two or more variables could be sought.

Disadvantages:

1. Actual effect of the second variable could not be obtained.
2. Could not use for studies concerned with learning. Because initial learning effect will be more and then only the plateau stage comes.

(iii) Repeated Measures Design

(Rotational Group Design) Another variation of single group design is the repeated measures design in this design all subjects in a group receive all treatments. This is used when several experimental treatments are to be investigated. Hence all subjects will be exposed to all treatments in a sequence. Here sufficient number of trials is given of the criterion task to all the subjects at the outset of the experiment in a deliberate attempt to cause learning to occur at an approximately equal extent.

The small amount of learning that may occur during the experiment can be tolerated by rotating the order of treatment administration by employing randomized order - Latin - square arrangement.

Order of Treatment

Group	I	II	III	IV	
	A	B	C	D	A- Baithak
	B	A	D	C	B-Stepping
	C	D	B	A	C-Leg thrust
	D	C	A	B	D-Alternative hopping

Eg. Effect of selected exercises on leg strength

Statistics: Analysis of variance and t-ratio are used.

Advantages

1. This could be used when several treatments are to be investigated.
2. This serves to control inter subject variability.
3. The cumulative effect of the treatments could be investigated.
4. Less subjects are needed
5. Less time is needed.

Disadvantages

1. The effect of each treatment could not be found out.
2. Not suitable for all types of research.
3. There is no control group to establish the effectiveness of the study.

2. MORE THAN ONE GROUP DESIGN

In this design two or more than two groups are used. The following three designs comes under this design.

(i) Static group comparison design

(ii) Random group design

(ii) Related group design

(i) Static Group Comparison Design

This group compares the status of a given that had experienced an experimental variables with a group that had not. In this design there is no experimentation and equivalence of grouping.

Example: The comparison of high school basketball players and non players on various physical and motor characteristics.

Procedure: A group of thirty college basketball players and thirty non players will be selected as subjects. Physical characteristics such as muscular strength, agility etc. may be found out for both the groups. Significant differences will be found.

Statistical Technique: t-test and analysis of variance.

Advantages: Very suitable to find out the physical and motor traits in growth studies.

Disadvantage: Not suitable for other types of studies.

(ii) Random Group Design

In this design, two or more groups are formed of subjects selected by random means. The experimental variable (factor) to be evaluated should also be randomly assigned to the various groups. If a control group is desired, one of the groups may be assigned as the control group by random means. The other group which undergoes the treatment is called as the experimental group. The control group would not receive any treatment. After a period of minimum six weeks both the groups will be tested on the criterion task. Significant difference will be noted.

Example: Effect of weight training on arm strength.

Procedure: Sixty students will be selected as subjects and divide them into groups (A&B) randomly. Assign group A as the experimental groups and B as a control group, randomly. The pre test will be conducted. For all the sixty students arm strength will be noted. Now for a minimum period of six weeks weight training will be given to the experimental group. The control group will not undergo any treatment. After the six weeks period again both the groups A and B post test will be conducted. Significant difference will be noted.

If more than one treatment is needed, additional groups may be included.

Advantages:

1. Since the control group is there the effectiveness could be established.

2. Any number of treatment groups can be established observation of several factors may be made.

Disadvantage:

Due to sampling process, the groups may have difference in initial performance (men). This initial mean difference may affect the corresponding difference in the final mean also.

Statistical Procedure:

Analysis of covariance and t-test are used to find out the significance.

3. RELATED GROUP DESIGN

This design is otherwise called as paired group design or equated group design or matched group design. In this, the subjects are divided into two groups on the basis of some initial trait. So that the groups equated placing of individuals with like scores in separate groups (process of matching or pairing). Hence the means and standard deviation of the test scores for each group will be the same. Now the treatment is administered to the experimental group for a period of six weeks and the control group does nothing. Now post test is taken to both (all) groups.

Example: Effect of weight training on the performance of shot put.

Procedure: If the researcher wishes to have only two groups, sixty subjects will be selected. All the sixty students pretest will be conducted and the shotput performance will be noted. Based on this performance arranging the like scores in different groups, the group will be made into two. The scores can be altered until the mean and standard deviation of both the groups are equal. Thus two equated groups are formed and now one is designed as experimental group and the other as control group. The experimental treatment of weight training is administrated to the experimental group and the control group does nothing. This is for a period of six weeks. After six weeks the post test will be conducted for both the groups. That is finding out the shotput performance. Now both the performance will be compared and the significance will be noted.

Statistical Procedure:

t-test (two groups) an analysis of variance (more than two groups) is used.

Advantages:

1. Since the control group is there the effectiveness of the experimental factor (variable) could be established.

2. Any number of treatment groups can be established. So that simultaneous observations of several factors may be made.

3. Since the process of matching is done, this is supposed to be the most suitable design.

Disadvantage:

No disadvantage.

MEANING OF EXPERIMENTAL RESEARCH

Experimental research is a method of research designed to determine influences both a qualitatively and quantitatively on a given phenomenon or to determine influence between or among variables.

Nature of Experimental Research

1. A good experimental research is one which provides the highest probability that the changes observed in the department variables are caused by manipulations of the independent variables.

2. The goal of experimental research is prediction and control.

3. The relationship between the treatment and the observed behavior is one of the reason-and-effects.

4. The nature of the reason-and-effect relationship enables the researcher to make statements which are predictive.

5. Good experimental design increases the probability that this assumption (hypothesis) is true.

6. Experimental study is a controlled study to control all influencing forces other than a variable which is manipulated under the controlled condition.

7. Precision is collection of data, use of instrument and doing statistics is very important.

8. Precision can be improved by selecting homogeneous group and also by increasing the accuracy of measurement.

PLANNING OF THE EXPERIMENTAL RESEARCH

1. Identification of Students:

Must be very careful in selecting the subjects for the research study. Eg: Age, sex, previous training, educational level etc. This depends on the type of the problem.

2. Specification of testing Equipment:

This include equipment such as goniometer, reaction timer, treadmill, computer, videotape, bicycle ergo meter, dynamometer etc. The necessary equipment must be available by the researcher. The researcher should have training experience to handle this equipment.

3. Procedure of the study:

The researcher should plan through procedure. That is regarding the limitation of the study and the method to be used to collect the data.

4. Experimental Design:

The researcher should plan the training schedule, number of days, and type of research design is going to follow.

Eg: Single group design or more than one group design.

5. Analysis and Interpretation:

Based on the statistics used the interpretation will be done. For this the researcher has to review allied topics and must get a broad knowledge about his research study.

5

Establishing and Development of Research

AREAS OF RESEARCH

Research in physical education and sport is multifarious and multifaceted. It encompasses a variety of problem areas that are character is typically peculiar in substance. The target proportion of research in physical education involves the experimental method, which uses a laboratory environment.

In order to conduct research setting up a research laboratory is an essentially. Aresearch laboratory is any room that is available to conduct experiments the basic prerequisite is that it permit one to obtain valid data. Even though there is so much of subject variety, a research laboratory for physical education and sport, now usually called the human performance laboratory. With a number of wings, the HPL must need cater to variety of research investigations under one roof.

There is no doubt that numerous research studies can be carried out on the play field itself. Yet appropriate space is needed where sophisticated instruments can be installed and also research studies are conducted under controlled conditions. There are certain field such as sports psychology, bio-chemistry, and bio-mechanics for which laboratory facility is a must to conduct research.

ESTABLISHING A RESEARCH LABORATORY

Research in physical education and sport is multifarious and multifaceted. It encompasses a variety of problem areas that are character is typically peculiar in substance. The target proportion of research in physical education involves the experiment methods, which uses a laboratory environment.

In order to conduct research setting up a research laboratory is an essentially. A research laboratory is any room that is available to conduct experiments; the basic prerequisite is that it permits on to obtain valid data. Even though there is so much of subject variety, a research laboratory for physical education and sports, now usually called the human performance laboratory. With a number of wings, the HPL must need cater to variety of research investigations under one roof.

There is no doubt that numerous research studies can be carried out on the play field itself. Yet appropriate space is needed where sophisticated instruments can be installed and also research studies are conducted under controlled conditions. There are certain field such as sports psychology, bio-chemistry, bio-mechanics for which laboratory facility is a must to conduct research.

Guide Lines for Establishing the Research Laboratory :

1. The status of an institution will greatly determine the dimension of a laboratory. For example; A national institute or a

university department with doctoral research facilities needs to have a highly developed laboratory than an ordinary physical education college.

2. The instruments for the laboratory depends upon the level of purpose of the research and finances available.

3. Competency of the research guiding personal plays an important role in establishing a laboratory of a high quality.

4. Setting up a research laboratory should be need based.

5. A laboratory should have technicians for proper maintenance and repair of instruments.

6. The laboratory atmosphere should be pollution free.

7. A laboratory should have sufficient electrical sockets and gadgets.

In institutions where adequate space, personal and funds are available, consideration must be given to the establishment of following laboratories.

1. Physical Laboratory

This laboratory should provide facilities for carrying out research on problems in the field of exercise physiology. In this laboratory there should be provision for sufficient electrical outlets so that different kinds of electronics and electrical instruments and apparatuses may be used for collection of data.

Reactions of man to environmental stresses, individual difference in functional ability and efficiency, cardio respiratory responses to activity stress at various age levels, calorimetory physiological performance tests and their validation are done in physiological laboratory. The following list of instruments may be considered as the minimum.

1. Tread mill
2. Bicycle ergometer
3. sphygmomanometer
4. Heart rate monitor
5. Expiro Graph
6. Gas Analyses (Both O_2 and CO_2)
7. Gaso meter
8. Baffle Chamber
9. Telechermo meter
10. Facility for hydrostatic weighing
11. Weighing machine
12. Stadio meter

In addition to the above list, if possible, the following instruments may also be provided.

1. Elctro – Cardio Graph
2. Cardiac stimulator
3. Count up and count down timer.

4. Telemetery receiver

5. Intra pulses

6. Mass spectrometer

7. Bio monitor

2. Anthropometry Lab

It is a branch of study which deals with body segments and their measurements. Describing body landmarks precisely, controlling the effects of extraneous variables affecting the process of measurement and the use of measuring instruments, classification of woman by body types, relationship of somatotype to various constitutional defects and diseases, racial differences in skeletal and muscle structure, skeletal maturity and physical performance, skeletal and muscular maturity, relationship between growth and strength and muscle hypertrophy. These are the areas of concern in laboratory research.

The anthropometry laboratory should have the following instruments.

1. Weight machine

2. Stadio meter

3. Measuring tape

4. Skinfold caliper

5. Anthropometer

6. Recumbent

7. Sliding caliper

8. Spreading caliper

3. Bio-mechanics Lab

This laboratory should have adequate facilities for the analysis of films taken on any aspects of physical education and sports. The following minimum equipment may be made available for research purpose.

1. Photo-Sonics high speed movie camera
2. Film projector
3. Digitizer with projection head
4. Mini computer cum projection head
5. Grip dynamo meter
6. Anthropometric kit
7. Gonio meter
8. Back and leg Dynamometer
9. Skinfold caliper
10. Tension meter

In addition to the above list if possible, the following instruments may also be provided.

1. Force Platform
2. E.M.C.

3. Photo electric timers

4. Video camera

5. Video cassette recorder

6. Movie camera

7. Manikin

In case adequate funds and facilities exits, provision must also be made for a photography laboratory for developing and printing films and enlarging prints both in black and white and in colour. In case a separate room is not available, a part of the motion analysis laboratory (preferably a corner of the laboratory) may be converted into a dark room for the purpose.

4. Psychology Lab

Experiments related to sportsmen's behavior are carried out in psychology laboratory.

This laboratory shall be established in a place which is quite and relatively free from traffic so that the subjects can concentrate while performing different tasks. To undertake research in this are, the following instruments may be provided in the laboratory.

1. Reaction and movement time apparatus

2. Human maze learning apparatus

3. Colour perception apparatus

4. Time sense apparatus

5. Depth perception apparatus

6. Hand steadiness apparatus

7. Apparatus for measuring horizontal – illusion.

8. Mirror drawing test.

9. Word reaction time apparatus

10. Two-hand co-ordination test.

11. Eye-hand co-ordination test.

12. Time conditional apparatus.

13. Reflex indicator

14. Skin resistance apparatus

15. Taschistoscope

16. Memory drum

17. Scales for measuring various psychological characteristics.

Apart from these laboratories a complete research laboratory should consist data analysis section to handle statistical analysis. This section should contain computer printer, type-writer and adequate number of pocket and table calculation with statistical functions. There should also be workshop to repair the instruments and to keep them in condition. The workshop should have necessary power tools and experience technical personnel. Besides these laboratories, adequate number of office rooms (preferably adjacent to each laboratory) for the research staff may be provided so that proper supervision is provided.

Computer Applications in Physical Education and Sports Research

Computer is a common term and popularly used in every days life. Computers are used in banks, office management, business applications, government offices, insurance, stock market, electricity department, printing and paper technology, engineering designs, meteorology, space technology, telephones, medicine, horoscope, entertainment, railways, traffic controls, transport department, defense, education and physical education is no exception.

Definition of computer

Computer is a machine. It possesses a memory and carry out given set of instructions instantaneously. The advantages of computer in management are speed, accuracy, imposes a discipline and versatile. A computer system includes interrelated elements such as microprocessor, keyboard, disk drive, and printer which are other wise called hardware. Different companies manufacture different types of computers, like mainframe computers, personal computers, and micro computers.

Computer can do very little without software. Software is the set of instructor that are operated through computers by using computer language. The most popular programming language are BASIC, COBAL, PASAL, FOTRAN, dBase, and 'C'.

Use of Computers in Research in Physical Education

The nature of Physical Education and sports has changed substantially during the recent past. It is enriched by different allied subject. There is already been exchange and extensive use of research material among these sciences. It is this educational intercourse that has led to the development of some new branches of knowledge like sports medicine, sports psychology, Bio-mechanics and etc. The entire concept of physical education and sports is changing at a rapid pace. The advantages derived from computers in the developed countries are amazing. We have to go a long way to understand and adept them in our situation.

Research scholars, physical education personnel need information. The principal research functions are planning, organizing, leading, deciding and evaluating are based on information. The areas of software application for research in physical education are word processing, database, spreadsheets, graphics, communications, personal information, and expert analysis.

Word Processing

There are many software programs designed for writing / entering the process of project work which allow the user enter text, it, saves it, print the next or communicate it to another, computer. Annual reports, inter collegiate, University, inter University Circulars, schedules of games and Sports may either stored or sent to concerned institutions through internet facility.

Database Program

This is one of the most useful programs for any research work or department of physical education. Storage and retrieval of large amounts of data in several combinations. For example: Sports equipment inventories, games team, injury records, participation records. Raw data from various tests could be entered for pre-established formulae to calculate desired results.

Communications

Increasingly important function of microcomputers perform today is through internet. E: mail messages could sent and message will reach other party instantaneously. Internet facility can help to go through the available literature, such as books, journals, magazines, and well during the research project. Physical education department can design a bulletin board system to provide information on upcoming events.

Spreadsheets

Software companies have created spreadsheets such as lotus 1-2-3 to manipulate numerical data with colums used for sports programs, preparing budget compiling teams and league matches. Any type of numerical data can be stored, manipulated and retrieved when necessary.

Graphics

Graphs refer to the visual effects that computers can create for on the screen display, printing pictures, and graphs which can be used several ways in research.

Research

Computers of great value to the research scholars in the field of physical education and sports. Programs can designed in the computers to create modules for experimental and research purposes which a student may use or discover for himself to find what happens in the given situation. The computer provides an opportunity for experiments which would not be possible in real life, because of dangers and cost. Computers can also be used in different set of dates, so that variety of conditions can be studied. One of the main feature of the computer is to process the data analysis. For example: as early as 1979 L. Cordins and S.C. Johnson research scholars in physical education from U.S.A. used computers in acquiring and evaluating respiratory and metabolic data generated from exercise.

Athletes, coaches, educators and sports scientist in advanced counties are familiar with he latest achievements in the field communication means, television, radio broadcasting and satellite communication. They have generated in all spheres of present – day life, including recreation, leisure, physical exercise and sports.

Computers haves played a vital role in improving athletes performance. Had Jesse Ownes run on a modern synthetic track, in lightweight running shoes, and with computers modules training, he would have produced much better timing than gold medal timing in Olympics. Computers cannot replace the biological factors for winning medals, but they can decide and monitor the oxygen intake which play vital role in distance runners. Sports scientists do reply more and more on computer modules to correct styles, analyze right body- weight and suggest corrective measures to improve performances.

The physio-diagnostic system which in designed by Dektor Schufried, an Australian Scholar provide an exact and detailed picture of the athlete's mental state in just ten minute and issues recommendations for it's correction. It is of particular importance in the process of intensive training. The computers not only determine the athlete's condition but also conducts a comprehensive in-depth examination, of his motor co-ordinations, power of mobilization, and response to stress. Computers are being used to elaborate the expert system involved in psychology of different sports.

The Thesis Report (or) Mechanism of Writing the Thesis Report

The findings of research must be reported so that the concerned people much as coaches, physical educationists etc... could become aware of the new professional field of knowledge.

A written format of a research work is known thesis or research report. The success of research scholar at any level mainly depends upon an orderly presentation of his thesis.

Thesis report consists of three main sections,

I. The preliminary section

II. The main body and

III. Reference section.

I. Preliminary Section

It consist of the following sections

1. Fly leaf
2. Title page
3. Certificate
4. Declaration
5. Dedication (Optional)
6. Vita (Optional)
5. Acknowledgement
8. Table of contents

List of tables
List of figures

II. The body of the Thesis

The main body of thesis contains 5 cap terns.

1. Introduction

2. Review of Related Literature

3. Methodology

4. Analysis and Interpretation of the Data.

5. Summary, Conclusions and Recommendations.

III. Reference Section:

Bibliography (or References)

Appendix (if any)

Index (if any)

I. Preliminary Material (or) Front Material

(i) Title page:

This page contains the name of the problem at the top (inverted pyramid form), the researcher's name in the center, the name of the institution, place and year at the bottom. The title should clearly indicate the subject, short, concise and correctly worded. Must be typed or printed with correct spelling.

(ii) Certificate page

Separate Certificate/approval sheet should be furnished immediately after the title page bearing that the thesis has not previously been formed on the basis of any degree, diploma, associateship, fellowship.

(iii) Decelaration

(iv) Dedication

Purely optional and personal matter. To indicate the names of the persons who have been a source of encouragement during the period of study. "TO MY"

The usual subject of dedication have been teachers, parents, wife husband and children.

(v) Vita

This gives adequate information to the reader regarding the researcher.

(a) Name of the researcher

(b) Place of birth

(c) Date of birth

(d) Undergraduate and graduate college attended

(e) Degrees awarded

(f) Areas of special interest

(g) Professional experience

(h) Awarded and Honours

(i) List of publications

(vi) Acknowledgement

The scholar would like to acknowledge her indebtedness to the thesis adviser, member of staff, friends, those who have been of considerable help in her research study. It should be simple and direct. Only the initials of the scholar will appear below the acknowledgement.

(vii) Table of Contents

Type in capitals and centered between the margins. 'chapter' and 'page' should be two double spaced below the main heading, 'table of contents'. Roman numerals are to be used indicating chapter numbers. Arabic numerals are used for page numbers. This must be aligned in such a manner that the last number of page is in line with the last letter 'e' of the word 'pages'. Main headings and sub heading should be clearly shown.

(viii) List of Tables

The word 'list of table' should be typed in capital letters and centered. The headings 'table and page' should have only the first letters capitalized. The table headings should be typed in small letters with the first letter and the important words capitalized. The listing of table headings should be three spaces below the main heading. There should be double space between headings.

(ix) List of Figures

It should include maps, drawings, diagrams, graphs, photographs etc… It should be typed in capital letters and centered between the side margins. The heading 'Figure'. The first letter of title only will start with capital and all the other in small letters.

II. Main Body of the Thesis

Chapter – I

(i) Introduction :

A short introductory statement leading to the problem. The nature of the problem also should come in the introduction.

(ii) Statement of the Problem:

The researcher should state the problem in the opening paragraph. The statement must cover the nature and type of the problem.

(iii) Significance of the Problem:

Reasons for taking up this study should be mentioned. What motivated him to take up this study and who is going to benefit from the study.

(iv) The Hypothesis:

This is intelligent and educated guess by the researcher about the result of the study. And it is a tentative answer to a question. An assumption based on the study. May be one or more hypotheses in one study.

(v) Limitation:

Items that show the restriction of the study. E.g. number of schools, library and duration (time). the conditions beyond the control of the investigator may be elaborated here. Eg. External factors like atmospheric pressure, temperature and resistance.

(vi) Delimitation:

The boundaries beyond which the study is not dealt with must be stated here. Brief idea about the restrictions made on such items as the number of variables, kind (children or adult or old), age, sex etc.

(vii) Definition of Technical Terms

All difficult or important terms used in the study should be defined and explained exactly in the manner they have been used in the study (for eg. Football refers to soccer or American football).

Chapter – II

(b) Review of Related Literature

A brief summary of previous research conducted, makes the researcher familiar with the background of the study. Closely related reviews help the researcher in making concepts clear helps to formulate the hypothesis and to understand the procedure.

Chapter – III

(c) Methodology or the procedure

This would give in detail the description of the types of research involved, i.e. the sample, number of variables selected, tools used method of collecting data and type of statistics used.

Chapter- IV

(d) Analysis and Interpretation of Data

This is the most important section of the research report. The actual analysis of the data and the derived results along with the findings and observations would come under this chapter. Tables and graphs will presented in the chapter.

Chapter - V

(e) Summary, Conclusion and Recommendation

(i) Summary:

This will present a brief abstract of the whole research study. A brief description about the problem, the procedure adopted and the findings.

(ii) Conclusions:

These are stated in specific terms and should provide explicit answer to questions posed in the problem.

(iii) Recommendations:

This helps for future studies. Theses are based on the data, result on personal judgement and experience of the researcher.

III. Reference Section :

Bibliography :

Bibliography is the last section of the thesis. It lists the relevant sources used by the research scholar in writing the thesis. These are classified in to sections and are divided into heads such as books, journals, un-published Thesis etc..and the entries should be arranged alphabetically under each head, using the surnamefirst.

Appendix :

Appendices may have some useful value for the understanding of the thesis. Appendices may include raw data, details of programmes, questionnaire, test forms, letters, list of individuals or institutions.

PREPARATION OF RESEARCH REPORT (Research Proposal)

Preparation proposal / synopsis

The research proposal / synopsis or an "It is general requirement out line of proposal work of most of the university beginning research. Serves as a useful basis for the evaluation of a project as will as guide line for the researcher.

Preparation of a research proposal or synopsis is an important step in the research process. It is the logical and systematic planning of a blue print or an out line which indicates the burden of study, its orientation, the methodology, the line of approach audits scope.

Types of Research Proposal

1. **Master and Degree**
2. **Master of Philosophy**
3. **Doctoral Degree**

This type of proposal is examined and evaluation by a committee of experts constituted by different institutions.

Parts of Research Proposal

1. The statement of the problem.
2. The significance of the problem.
3. Definitions, Limitations and Delimitations.
4. Review of related literature.
5. The Hypothesis.
6. Methodology.
7. Bibliography.
8. Time and Budget schedule.

ABSTRACT

A summary of research report of thesis is prepared in the form of abstract. It provides the brief description of main points of research report. The main theme is given in the abstract of a research work. A well written abstract of a research to every one who is going through research process.

Generally a researcher has to prepare an abstract after completing his research thesis or report.

Usually Reasearch Abstact Consists of Three Main Parts:

1. Introduction
2. Main body of the report and
3. Conclusions.

1. The introducing part empresses the significance the problem, objectives and hypothesis of the study.
2. It includes methods sampling techniques, analysis and result of the study. The last part provides contributions and discussions of the study.
3. The implication of the findings are also highlighted at the end.

The structure of the report is also given light most important references are also written in the form of bibliography. The report is written in past tense and in the third period.

Based on the purpose, abstract takes various formats. They are :

1. Thesis or dissertation abstract.
2. Abstract for published papers.
3. Conference abstract.

Index